EXTREME sports

snowboarding

W
FRANKLIN WATTS
NEW YORK • LONDON • SYDNEY

contents

Snowboarding is the newest and most exciting sport on the mountains today.

It started back in the 1960s. Surfers from California wanted to try out their skills on the snow.

There are now three types of boarding –

⬭ **freeriding**
⬭ **freestyling**
⬭ **racing**

Snowboarding is easy to learn and great fun to do. It is not about fashion. It's not going to fade away. It's here to stay. Enjoy yourself, ride safely and ...

3 *be free*

freeriding

Freeriding means using the whole mountain as a playground. Ride through trees, over cliffs ... whatever comes your way.

freestyling

Freestyling is about doing tricks and stunts. It's like skateboarding, but on the ramps and halfpipes of the mountains.

MAIN PHOTO BY A FOUR

Halfpipe

A halfpipe is a man-made ramp, shaped like a 'U'. Snowboarders ride up the sides of the halfpipe, jumping out and doing tricks.

racing

Racing is the nearest you'll get to skiing on a board. The riders try to go as fast as possible down the slope. There are two types of race –

Slalom

Two riders race against each other. Both riders have their own course. The two courses are next to each other.

Giant slalom

This is a race against the clock. The riders make larger and faster turns than in slalom racing.

the right board

Getting the right board is vital. There are many different styles, so it can be difficult to know which one to go for. It will depend on your size and height and what kind of snowboarding you want to do. A good snowboard shop will help you choose the right one for all your needs.

BOARD PHOTOS BY BURTON

freestyle

These boards are wider and softer than other boards. The nose (front) and tail (back) of the board are the same shape. This is so they can ride fakie (backwards) as easily as forwards.

freeride

These are narrower and stiffer than freestyle boards. They have a longer, up-turned nose so they can ride through fresh, powdery snow easily.

racing

Racing boards are the narrowest and stiffest of all the boards. They have a flat tail because they are built to go forwards only.

nose

tail

boots and bindings

The bindings clip you and your boots to the board. Again, there are different types for the different styles of boarding.

Once you're strapped in, the side of the board nearest your toes becomes the 'toeside edge'. The side nearest your heels is the 'heelside edge'.

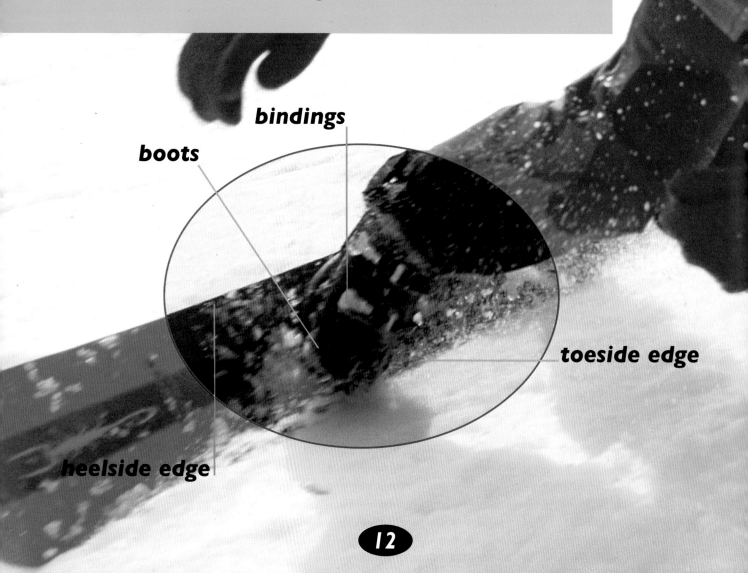

bindings

boots

toeside edge

heelside edge

freestyle/freeride

These boots are soft with laces at the front. Freeride boots give a little more support than freestyle. The bindings are plastic and have two or three clips to hold the boots.

racing

These boots have a hard plastic shell. The bindings are also hard. They clip onto the toe and heel of the boot.

step-ins

These allow you to 'step-in' and 'step-out' of your board without the need for clips.

13

snowboard clothing

The clothes you wear should keep you warm and dry when you're on the mountain. Snowboard clothing also has its own style. It has a loose look, like skate and surf wear.

Trousers and jackets

Trousers and jackets need to be tough and waterproof. They should be loose to allow you to move freely. Extra padding is often put into the seat and knees of the trousers to stop you getting bruised.

Gloves

Gloves should have a high cuff to keep snow out. They also need extra padding around the fingers.

Hats

A wool beanie will help keep the heat in your body.

Glasses and goggles

Goggles will stop the snow flying up into your eyes. Glasses and goggles will protect your eyes from the sun. You should also wear sun cream on your face.

Underclothing

Thermal underwear and fleece jumpers are great for warmth. Wear a few layers to keep the heat in.

where to start

Even if you don't live in an area that has snow, you can still enjoy the thrill of boarding. There are many dry slopes where you can learn all the skills. There are also holidays especially for boarders where you can hire all the gear.

Over the next few pages we'll give you tips on some of the basic moves that every rider needs to know. But everyone should also have proper lessons from an instructor. It's the best way to learn. They will also teach you how to ride safely on the mountains.

PHOTO TOP RIGHT BY A FOUR

very basic

stuff

Regular or goofy?

Choose whether to stand with your left foot forwards (regular) or your right foot forwards (goofy). See which one feels more comfortable.

Left: A regular rider with his front foot clipped in.

basic stance

Try out your basic standing position (stance). Put your board on the flat so it won't move. Clip in both feet. You should be relaxed. Bend your legs slightly. Let your hips and upper body face the same way as your front foot. Hold your arms out slightly to help you balance. Keep your weight equal on both feet.

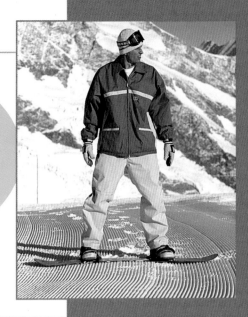

heelside moves

A heelside move is any move where you are using the heelside edge of your board. To do this, just lean back on your heels. Bend your legs slightly.

The heelside edge of your board will grip the slope. This will help you control your speed as you move.

toeside moves

Instead of leaning on your heels, just bend your legs and lean towards your toes. This time, your toeside edge will be gripping the slope. You must practise all moves on your heelside and your toeside edge.

swing to the hill

This is your first taste of turning. It's a simple curve across the slope.

Start in the basic position. Put more weight on your front foot.

1 *Point the nose of the board down the slope. You will start to move forwards.*

2 *Steer the board across the slope by turning the top half of your body. Lean on your toes.*

You can stop by sliding the board across the slope.

This is a toeside swing to the hill.
To turn the other way, do the
move on your heelside edge.

the whole turn

To get down the whole slope, you'll need to be able to link your turns.

1 *Keep your upper body facing the same way as your front leg. Keep the weight on your front leg.*

2 *Keep your body loose and relaxed. Hold out your arms to help you balance. Bend your legs.*

2

3

3 *Stand up slightly.*
Turn the top half of
your body the way
you want to go.

4 *Lean forwards on your toes as*
you go across the hill.
Get ready to turn the other way.

5 *Stand up and make the turn.*

6 *Lean back on your heels. Carry*
on until you fall over.

6

Turn the page to find out about ollie grabs.

the ollie

1

2

Once you've got the basics, you'll want to go on to try a few tricks. The ollie is a simple jump. You can use it on flat ground or to help you get more height when you jump from a ramp.

Lean back on the tail of your board.
Pull up your front foot.
Push up off the ground with your back foot.

 Once in the air, pull your feet up underneath you.
Try to keep the board flat.

 Land with your weight over the middle of
the board.

4 Bending your legs will help you to land smoothly.

tricks plus

Indie

Tail grab

After the ollie, there are many other tricks to learn. A lot of them involve grabbing a part of the board when you make a jump (known as 'ollie grabs').

We can't show you all of them, but here are some of the simplest.

Mute
Hold your toeside edge with your front hand.

Tail grab
Reach back and grab the tail of your board.

Indie
Use your back hand to grab the toeside edge of your board.

Method
Hold your heelside edge with your front hand.

powder riding

Riding through fresh, powdery snow is one of the best feelings that snowboarding can give you. It's also easy to learn.

Start off in snow that isn't too deep. About 12 to 15 centimetres is enough to get the feel. Make smooth turns as normal. Lean back a little on the tail of your board to stop the nose from sinking. If you put the bindings a few centimetres closer to the tail it will be easier.

 extreme snowboarding

Extreme snowboarding is freeriding in the most dangerous parts of the mountain.

For the experts only.

extra stuff

Disclaimer

In the preparation of this book all due care has been exercised with regard to the activities depicted. The Publishers regret that they can accept no liability for any loss or injury sustained.

Text: Becci Malthouse
(Becci is a British Snowboarding
Association-approved snowboard trainer)
Photos: Sang Tan (except where indicated)

Series editor: Matthew Parselle
Art director: Robert Walster
Designer: Andy Stagg
Reading consultant: Frances James

This edition published in 2000 by Franklin Watts
© Franklin Watts 1997

Franklin Watts
96 Leonard Street
London EC2A 4RH
A CIP catalogue for this
book is available from
the British Library.

Franklin Watts Australia
14 Mars Road
Lane Cove NSW 2066
ISBN 0 7496 2772 7 (Hb)
     0 7496 3610 6 (Pb)
Dewey classification 796.93

Printed in Great Britain

Index